Sonny St

MW00812191

IMPROVISED TENOR SAXOPHONE SOLOS
TRANSCRIBED & EDITED BY GARY KELLER

TABLE OF CONTENTS

FROM THE ALBUM

INTRODUCTION

Edward "Sonny" Stitt was born in Boston, Mass. in 1924. He came from a musical family, his father being a college music professor and his brother a concert pianist. After working around Newark and Detroit, Stitt toured with the Tiny Bradshaw Band, then moved to New York City in 1945. With the exception of short stints with Dizzy Gillespie and Miles Davis, Stitt led his own combos or was featured as a guest soloist with local rhythm sections. He also appeared with Gene Ammons, performing and recording as the "Boss Tenors." Sonny Stitt was one of the most recorded saxophonists in jazz and many of his records are still available. The selected discography contained in this book is an excellent representation of his strongest albums.

Most saxophonists in the forties were influenced by Charlie Parker, and Stitt was no exception. In fact, many consider his switch to tenor sax as his primary instrument an attempt to shed the image of a Bird disciple. However, to dismiss Stitt's style as solely derived from Bird would be unfair. Considering his background, Stitt undoubtedly would have developed much the same style even if he had never heard Parker. His grasp on the concepts of modern jazz was unquestionably first hand.

Sonny Stitt's tenor sax style was very reminiscent of Lester Young, especially evidenced in his preference for a lighter sound and his "laid-back" time feel. Stitt's frequent use of alternate fingerings to change a note's color or provide rhythmic effect can also be traced back to Young. His harmonic concept, however, is clearly derived from "modern jazz." Note his use of the altered tones of the dominant seventh, the diminished scale, and his extensive use of double time lines. Stitt's tenor playing was a strong influence on many subsequent players, most notably John Coltrane. Careful examination of the "Green Dolphin Street" solo will reveal many motifs found in Coltrane's mid-1950's recordings.

Although Stitt used all of the common harmonic and melodic devices of the bebop and hard bop eras, his playing contained very little "change running" or playing chords only for chord's sake. He often implied substitute progressions but did so with melody as well as chord arpeggiation. His strength was his ability to string together chorus after chorus of logical, concise melodies with remarkable rhythmic precision. Most players would be hard pressed to individually compose so many flawless choruses, much less improvise them on the spot.

From an educational standpoint, Sonny Stitt's solos are helpful in many ways. They are relatively easy to read and demand somewhat less technical ability than the solos of other players, yet they surpass most in terms of accurate note choices and melodic continuity. The link between harmony and improvised melody seems especially clear in Stitt's playing, and studying several "licks" will help the student gain some conceptual awareness of how improvised lines are conceived.

The student should use this book in conjunction with the recorded solos. Playing along with the record is the only way to gain insight into the nuances of phrasing, articulation, rhythmic feel, etc.. If the recordings are unavailable, pay close attention to the marked articulations and try to generate a strong, triplet oriented eighth note feel. This will bring you close to Stitt's style. Be sure to consult the chord changes and study Stitt's methods of turning these harmonic guidelines into string melodies.

If the student is not already familiar with basic scales (major, minors, whole tone and diminished), modes (especially dorian and mixolydian), and fundamental harmony, I strongly suggest Jerry Coker's **Improvising Jazz** (Prentice Hall) and **Patterns For Jazz,** (Studio P/R-Columbia).

ABOUT THE EDITOR

Gary Keller is currently the Professor of Saxophone at the University of Miami in Coral Gables, Florida. He has studied saxophone with Lawrence Wyman (S.U.N.Y. Fredonia), John Sedola (Buffalo, New York), Kirby Campbell (University of Miami), and Joe Allard (New York, N.Y.). He has studied jazz improvisation with David Liebman, Pat LaBarbera, and Bob Mover. He has a Master's Degree in Jazz Performance from the University of Miami.

In addition to his teaching duties, Mr. Keller is active in the Miami night club and showroom scene, playing for many of the name acts traveling through Miami. He also co-leads a jazz quintet with fellow faculty member Ron Miller. His past experience includes a stint with the Woody Herman Orchestra (1980-81).

PRACTICE TIPS

1. Using a metronome to beat on the 2nd and 4th beats of each bar duplicates the feeling of playing with a drummers hi-hat cymbal.

2. If you do not instantly recognize how each note functions in the chord progression, write an analysis of the solo. Label each note (passing tone ♭9, ♯11, 3rd, etc.) according to its usage. Also look for scales and scale segments (dorian, diminished, altered, etc.).

3. Tranpose your favorite phrases into other keys, especially ii-V7-I phrases.

4. **Memorize** the solos and the changes of the tunes!

5. Pay close attention to Stitt's interpretation of each tune's melody.

6. Conciencious, in depth study of one solo will be of more benefit than a casual reading of the entire book. Be sure to absorb as much as you can from each solo before going onto the next.

TABLE OF ABBREVIATIONS

*	Indicates use of "la" tongue for tonal contrast
___	Indicates note is held full value
·	Indicates note played short but not accented
∧	Indicates note played short and accented
♩ or ♫ or ♭♩	Indicates lip bend of combination lip and finger bend if seen accompanied by a grace note
①	Circled number indicates top of an improvised chorus (beginning after statement of the melody)
S	Indicates note played with the appropriate side key(s)
+	Indicates some nature of "false" fingering described in detail at the end of the first solo in which it occurs
(A - 7)	Chord changes appearing in brackets above solo indicate an implied change from the harmony used for the melody. Also used to indicate ghosted notes or notes unclear on recording
♪⌒ or ♩)	Indicates short fall at end of note
>	Accented and held full value

SELECTED STITT DISCOGRAPHY*

A Little Bit of Stitt, Roost 2235**
Boss Tenors Straight Ahead From Chicago, Verve V8426
Bud's Blues, Prestige 7839
Constellation, Cobblestone 9021
Dizzy Gillespie: The Sonny Stitt/Sonny Rollins Sessions, Verve VEZ 2505
Genesis, Prestige T 24044
So Doggone Good, Prestige 10074
Sonny's Blues, Phoenix PHX 308
Sunnyside Up, Roost 2245
Sonny Stitt, Marble Arts MAL 753
Sonny Stitt With The New Yorkers, Roost 2226
Soul Electricity, Prestige 7635
Stitt Meets Brother Jack, Prestige 7244
Stittsville, Roost 2244
Tune Up, Cobblestone 9013

* Sonny Stitt was a particularly consistent performer and virtually all his records are of value. This list represents my personal favorites.

** Most Roost records are now out of print. They can be found in used record stores, etc, and are well worth hunting for.

6

STELLA BY STARLIGHT

FROM "SOUL ELECTRICITY" PRESTIGE # 7635

By
NED WASHINGTON
and VICTOR YOUNG

8

(VAMP ENDING ST. 8TH's)

TAG

(VAMP) (ST. 8TH FEEL)
Ama   D7(13)

+ INDICATES THE FOLLOWING "FALSE" FINGERINGS:

C#: PLAY LOW C# WITH OCTAVE KEY
    JUST OVERBLOW 1 OCTAVE

D: ADD SIDE D TO REGULAR (LONG) D FINGERING

(Eb)
D# : ADD BOTH SIDE D AND Eb TO REGULAR Eb FINGERING

STELLA BY STARLIGHT

| D#ø | G#⁷ | Bmi⁷ | E⁷ |

| Emi⁷ | A⁷ | D | Dmi⁷ G⁷ |

| A⁶ | D#ø G#⁷ | C#mi | Ami⁷ D⁷ |

| E | D#ø G#⁷ | G#ø | C#⁷(b9) |

| F#+⁷ | | Bmi⁷(11) | |

| G⁷ | | A | |

| D#ø | G#⁷(b9 b13) | C#ø | F#⁷(b9 b13) |

| Cmi⁷ F⁷ | Bmi⁷ E⁷ | A | |

IT COULD HAPPEN TO YOU

FROM "STITTSVILLE" ROOST 2244

By
JOHNNY BURKE
and JAMES VAN HEUSEN

+ USE THIS FINGERING FOR B♭ AND A WA-WA UP MOVEMENT.
   (A TREMOLO BETWEEN G+B♭ WILL RESULT.)

E♭

IT COULD HAPPEN TO YOU

ON GREEN DOLPHIN STREET
FROM "SUNNY SIDE UP"

By
NED WASHINGTON
and BRONISLAU KAPER

PIANO SOLO

(LATIN)

ON GREEN DOLPHIN STREET

JUST YOU, JUST ME

FROM "SONNY STITT"   MARBLE ARTS #753

By
RAYMOND KLAGES
and JESSE GREER

LAY BACK

JUST YOU, JUST ME

OVER THE RAINBOW

FROM "SOUL ELECTRICITY" PRESTIGE 7635

By
E.Y. HARBURG
and HAROLD ARLEN

8TH NOTES PLAYED IN A STRAIGHT STYLE

OVER THE RAINBOW

ALL INSTRUMENTS - JAZZ AND IMPROVISATION

- **12 Keys To Jazz Concepts/Chuck Marohnic** (SB200)
- **Basic Jazz Improvisation-Bb Book** (SB242)
- **A Complete Method for Jazz Improvisation/ Jerry Coker** (SB84)
- **Everybody Can Play The Blues/Hamilton** (SB172)
- **Drones For Improvisation/ Coker-Norris** (SB253)

Jazz Duets (for all treble clef instruments)
- **(Reyman)** (SB111)
- **(Polansky)** (SB112)
- **Jazz Keyboard for Pianists and Non-Pianists/Coker** (SB284)

- **(The) Jazz Language (A Theory Text For Jazz Composition and Improvisation) by Dan Haerle** (SB75)
- **Legit Etudes For The Jazz Oriented Player/Carubia & Drewes** (SB254)
- **Lookout Farm-Small Group Improvisation Case Study** (GXF4059)
- **The Mixed Modal Approach To Contemporary Improvisation/Joseph V. Tranchina** (SB71)

New Concepts In Linear Improvisation/Ramon Ricker
- **Textbook** (SB32)
- **Workbook & Cassette** (SB33)

Charlie Parker Omnibook
- **For B-Flat Instruments** (SBO118)
- **For C Instruments** (SBO117)
- **For E-Flat Instruments** (SBO116)

Patterns For Jazz/Coker, Casale, Campbell and Greene
- **For Bass Clef Instruments** (SB72)
- **For Treble Clef Instruments** (SB1)

- **Pentatonic Scales For Jazz Improvisation/Ramon Ricker** (SB9)

Ramon Ricker Improvisation Series
(see display)

- **Scales For Jazz Improvisation (A Practice Method For All Instruments)/Dan Haerle** (SB7)
- **Singer's Jam Session/P. Coker (includes two tapes)** (SB251)

Stretching Out/Dominic Spera
- **Bass Clef Book** (SJ8104)
- **B-Flat Book** (SJ8103)
- **C Book** (SJ8101)
- **E-Flat Book** (SJ8102)
- **Rhythm Section Book** (SJ8106)
- **Cassette** (SJ8100)

- **Technique Development In Fourths For Jazz Improvisation/Ramon Ricker** (SB17)

NOW 'EAR THIS

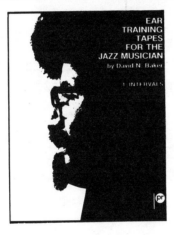

- **A NEW APPROACH TO EAR TRAINING FOR JAZZ MUSICIANS (SB18)**

By David N. Baker. Includes two cassettes. A comprehensive method that will develop the ear training skills necessary for the professional jazz musician. David Baker has put together literally a thesaurus of scales and chords. A step-by-step approach that is pertinent for improvisational study and transcribing of recorded solos, there is also a wealth of preparatory exercises on the accompanying cassette tapes. Exercise answers are played or sung back by "ear" rather than being written down, which helps a student correlate what he "hears," no matter which instrument he plays. Use the tapes and text with any instrument. The discography is an excellent source for study, as record cuts by noted jazz artists on selected albums are identified by the scales they use predominately in the solos. An exemplary method in jazz pedagogy heartily recommended for intermediate or advanced players.

- **ADVANCED EAR TRAINING FOR JAZZ MUSICIANS (SB34)**

By David N. Baker. 68 pages and cassette for the serious jazz musician. Working with scales and chords, the jaz player moves into new areas of performance — Baker sets up exercises for student and soloist to build confidence and expertise.

EAR TRAINING TAPES FOR THE JAZZ MUSICIAN
By David N. Baker. Five progressive volumes, each one containing a book and a cassette. Tips and steps for developing the ear - exercises dealing with specific recognitions.
- **No. 1 - Intervals** (SB120)
- **No. 2 - Triads, Three Note Sets, Four & Five Note Sets** (SB121)
- **No. 3 - Seventh Chords, Scales** (SB122)
- **No. 4 - Major Melodies Turnarounds, I-VI7, Formulae** (SB123)
- **No. 5 - Patterns** (SB124)

JAZZ TUNES FOR IMPROVISATION
By Dan Haerle, Jack Petersen & Rich Matteson. A collection of 67 tunes covering the full range of styles and harmonies.
- **For B-flat Instruments** (SB109)
- **For E-flat Instruments** (SB110)
- **For C Instruments** (SB107)
- **For Bass Clef Instruments** (SB108)

CASSETTE TAPES FOR JAZZ TUNES FOR IMPROVISATION
Each text is divided into 4 sections (some sections require two tapes). Get the whole book (7 pages) or do one section at a time. The same tape is used with all 4 instrument books.
- **Complete Set (7 tapes)** (SBT830)
- **Section I, Tape 1** (SBT831)
- **Section II, Tape 1** (SBT832)
- **Section II, Tape 2** (SBT833)
- **Section III, Tape 1** (SBT834)
- **Section III, Tape 2** (SBT835)
- **Section IV, Tape 1** (SBT836)
- **Section IV, Tape 2** (SBT837)